Draft Environmental Assessment

Blanco County
Church Tank Tower Site
Blanco County, Texas

Homeland Security Grant Program (HSGP)
Project # 2010-SS-T0-0008 (9897)

October 2011

 FEMA

Federal Emergency Management Agency
Department of Homeland Security
500 C Street, SW
Washington, DC 20472

Table of Contents

Appendixes

    Appendix A: Site Photographs

    Appendix B: Site Location Maps

    Appendix C: Agency Consultation Letters

    Appendix D: NEPA Summary Report and Checklist

1.0 Introduction

Blanco County, Texas has been awarded, under the Federal Emergency Management Agency (FEMA) Homeland Security Program Grant (HSGP) authorization to construct a three hundred (300) foot new communications tower, a total of three hundred twenty (320) feet with the planned attached antennae. This communications tower will enhance the interoperable communications among all first responder disciplines in response to terrorist attacks and during times of natural or man-made disasters.

The HSGP provides grant funding to public safety agencies for the protection of critical communications infrastructure from terrorism, natural disasters and routine operations. HSGP supports the implementation of State Homeland Security Strategies to address the identified planning, organization, equipment, training, and exercise needs to prevent, protect against, respond to, and recover from acts of terrorism and other catastrophic events.

This Environmental Assessment (EA) has been prepared according to the requirements of the National Environmental Policy Act (NEPA), as applied to the Federal Emergency Management Agency (FEMA) at 44 CFR Part 10. This section of the federal code requires that FEMA take into account environmental considerations when authorizing or approving actions, pursuant to the National Environmental Policy Act.

This phased project, is a joint venture between Burnet (1,021 Sq. Mi.), Llano (966 Sq. Mi.) and Blanco (713 Sq. Mi.) Counties will build a P25 Regional VHF Digital Trunking Communications System that allows for a link back to the Austin Master Site Controller making it an element of a much larger Capital Area Council of Governments (CAPCOG) Regional Radio System. The terrain of the three counties consists of 2,700 Square Miles of rural, rugged hills, valleys, and lakes over the three county areas. The new system will increase coverage from non-existent in numerous locations to approximately 94% AREA Portable Inbound coverage. (See Appendix B, Coverage Studies Performed April 2009).

The Project is being installed in Phases beginning with FY 2007 Grant Year thru FY 2010 Grant Year. The link back to the Austin Master Site Controller making it an element of a much larger CAPCOG Regional Radio System is being planned for FY 2011 Grant Year. This project will assist Burnet, Llano and Blanco Counties in completing our P25 Communications System for our CAPCOG Regional Interoperable project and is fully compliant with the Federal Communications Commission (FCC) January 1, 2013 Narrowband mandate for VHF Frequencies. In support of the proposed project, the Blanco County Commissioners Court conducted a public meeting on August 9, 2011 that included discussions regarding the funding for the Round Mountain Tower site (Appendix C).

The purpose of this EA is to analyze the potential environmental impacts of the proposed construction of a communications tower facility. FEMA will use the findings in this EA to determine whether to prepare an Environmental Impact Statement (EIS) or a Finding of No Significant Impact (FONSI).

2.0   Purpose and Need

The area to be serviced by this project is located within Blanco County, Texas. The site for the construction of the proposed communications tower is on property acquired by Blanco County from the City of Blanco. A portion of the adjacent tract of land currently houses a public water storage tank and existing radio communications tower for the City of Blanco.

A National Priority of the 2009 HSGP as per FY2009 Grant Guidance is to "strengthen chemical, biological, radiological/nuclear, and explosive detection, response, and decontamination. Statewide interoperable communications is integral to the accomplishment of this priority and all other National Priorities. This new regional communications tower is needed in Blanco County to improve public safety and interoperable communications among emergency responders during such an emergency event.

3.0   Alternatives

Alternative No. 1- No Action

Under this alternative, the tower would not be constructed. This alternative jeopardizes public safety because communications among emergency responders would be impossible during an emergency event. The existing communications system is inadequate due to the terrain, specifically, the 2,700 square miles of rural, rugged hills, valleys, and lakes over the three-county area. The consequences of not implementing the construction of this project will cause Burnet, Llano, and Blanco Counties to be non-compliant with the FCC January 1, 2013 Narrowband mandate for VHF Frequencies and would severely impact the Regional Radio System for Public Safety. Without this project, Blanco County cannot meet the Department of Homeland Security interoperable communications mandates.

Alternative No. 1- Proposed Action

The proposed site is located along 3944 US 281 South in Blanco County, Texas 78663 (Latitude: 30.046583, -Longitude:-98.410639) (Appendix A and B). This tower is one of the last two towers needed to complete the Regional Radio System for Public Safety in this three county area of Texas. The proposed Church Tank Tower Height is 320 feet above ground level (AGL) and 1,497 feet above mean sea level (AMSL). This will be a self-supporting lighted tower structure. The tower will be painted and lighted with white strobe and red strobe lights in accordance to Federal Aviation Administration (FAA) guidelines. Ground disturbance for new construction and structure modification including trenching for utility lines, installation of fencing and light posts, tower footing and pads, etc. will be minimal and are estimated to be 145 feet x 85 feet or less than (1/3) acre for the Church Tank Tower Site. The trenching for utility lines will be approximately 24 inches in depth x 20 feet in length, installation of fencing approximately 24 inches to 36 inches in depth, the tower footings will be approximately 3 feet in diameter x 21 inches in depth x 3 and pads 20 feet in length x 12 feet wide.

4.0   Alternatives Considered and Dismissed

Three alternative sites were considered but dismissed because they did not meet the County's purpose and need, and were considered not feasible, based on engineering studies to meet communications requirements.

Alternative Site #1 was considered and dismissed due to the rugged hills, valleys, and lakes. Based on engineering studies, the Coverage Studies Map dated April 2, 2009 reflected that the coverage for the desired area could not be achieved to meet communications requirements.

Alternative Site #2 was considered and dismissed due to the tower height requirement necessary to clear the mountain ridge and the amount of grant money received for the project. This alternative would have required a guyed tower structure and caused Mitigation measures that were not achievable as with the lighted freestanding lattice type tower structure recommended guidelines for minimal impact to bird fatalities.

Alternative Site #3 was considered and dismissed due to the rugged hills and the distance between the tower sites. It was not possible to cover the large distances and achieve the communication requirements with the available equipment due to the limitation of maximum distance between physical site locations.

5.0   Geology, Soils, and Seismicity

Under the No Action alternative, there would be no short- or long-term impacts to soils, geologic resources, or seismic features.

The native soil profile revealed a layer of clay underlain by intact limestone bedrock with interbedded weathered layers. Local geology maps and boring samples indicate the presence of the Glen Rose Formation, the youngest formation of the Trinity Group from Lower Cretaceous Period, forming a narrow prairie from Austin northwest to the project. It is predominately a limestone formation, typically consisting of thin to massively bedded, hard limestone strata alternating with clay, argillaceous limestone and thin sandstone strata. There is also presence of reddish brown clay, light yellowish brown clay with limestone fragments, limestone pale brown severely weathered with thick to vary hard layers, limestone gray hard to very hard, limestone pale brown severely weathered with thick hard to very hard layers, and limestone gray hard to very hard.

The elevation is approximately 1,497 feet AMSL. The site consists of gently sloping topography with natural slopes ranging up to approximately 4 percent. There are no published indications of faults in the vicinity of the site. No groundwater was identified during the site investigations. The vegetation on the site consists mainly of grasses and no trees. The fenced tower and equipment compound will co-locate. Adjacent undeveloped areas are not expected to be impacted.

Ground disturbance would be confined to the boring of the tower footings, electrical lines, equipment shelter foundation, and fencing. The proposed footings are cement in nature, and will be approximately three (3) to four (4) feet in diameter, and thirty (30) to forty (40) feet in depth. If necessary, surface runoff will be controlled by using biodegradable barriers such as hay bales to minimize erosion. Proper disposal of any hazards will be utilized. Therefore, the Proposed Action will not impact geologic resources and will not have significant impacts to soils.

6.0   Water Resources

Under the No Action alternative, there would be no short- or long-term impacts to water resources.

The National Pollutant Discharge Elimination System (NPDES) was established under the Clean Water Act and regulates wastewater discharges from point sources. NPDES regulations require that construction sites resulting in greater than one acre of disturbance obtain a permit from the Environmental Protection Agency (EPA), or the corresponding state agency where the permitting role has been assumed by the state. In Texas, the Texas Commission on Environment Quality is the state agency that has assumed this responsibility. Land-disturbing activities at the proposed communication tower facility will be below the one-acre threshold requiring an NPDES permit.

There are no bodies of water located on the project site. If necessary, surface runoff will be controlled by using biodegradable barriers such as hay bales to minimize erosion. Any hazardous material used or encountered during construction will be handled per local, state, and federal regulations. Therefore, the Proposed Action would have no significant impacts to water quality in the area of the site.

7.0   Wetlands

Under the No Action alternative, there would be no short- or long-term impacts to wetlands.

Under the Clean Water Act (40 CFR 230.3), and Executive Order 11990, wetlands are defined as "those areas that are inundated or saturated by surface or ground water at a frequency and duration sufficient to support, and that under normal circumstances do support, a prevalence if

4

vegetation typically adapted for life in saturated conditions. Wetlands generally include swamps, marshes, bogs and similar areas." Based on the United States Fish and Wildlife Services (USFWS) National Wetlands Inventory map available online at the National Wetlands Inventory website (http://fws.gov/wetlands/), no wetland were identified in the project area (Appendix B). The proposed communication tower site consists of gently sloping topography with natural slopes ranging up to approximately 4 percent. The vegetation on the site consists mainly of grasses and one oak tree on the tower site, and sparsely situated oak trees near the precinct barn. None of the plant species are indicative of vegetation associated with wetlands. No ground water or surface water was identified on the site. All wetland indicators were absent from this site. Therefore, the Proposed Action will not impact wetlands.

8.0   Floodplain

Under the No Action alternative, there would be no short- or long-term impacts to floodplains.

Printed floodplain maps are not available for this region of Texas. However, based on FEMA's internal GIS flood data, this site is located in Zone X (panel # 48031C0105C, dated February 6, 1991) and outside the 100 (or 500) year flood zone. Therefore, the Proposed Action would not impact or be impacted by the 100-year floodplain.

9.0   Coastal Resources

Under the No Action alternative, there would be no short- or long-term impacts to coastal resources.

The Coastal Zone Management Act (CZMA) was established in 1972 to preserve, protect, and (where possible) restore or enhance the resources of the coastal zones of the United States.

The proposed project is not located within and has no impact on coastal resource areas. Therefore, the Proposed Action does not require a coastal use permit.

10.0 Wild and Scenic Rivers

Under the No Action alternative, there would be no short- or long-term impacts to Wild and Scenic Rivers.

A review of information available through the www.rivers.gov website indicates that there are no bodies of water located on or adjacent to the project site.

The proposed communications tower would have no impacts to any designated Wild and Scenic Rivers.

11.0 Threatened and Endangered Species and Critical Habitat

Under the No Action alternative, there would be no short- or long-term impacts to Threatened and Endangered Species or Critical Habitat.

Section 7 of the Endangered Species Act of 1973 (16 U.S.C. 1536a2) directs Federal agencies to utilize their authorities in furtherance of the purposes of the Act by carrying out programs for the conservation of listed species or designated critical habitats. In addition, Section 7 of the Act sets out the consultation process, which is further implemented by regulation (50 CFR 402). According to the USFWS Threatened and Endangered Species System website (http://www.fws.gov/endangered/), threatened or endangered species are known to exist in Blanco County, Texas.

The Whooping Crane (*Grus Americana*) is listed as an endangered bird species. The habitat of the whooping crane population documented in Texas extends from Wood Buffalo National Park to Aransas National Wildlife Refuge on the Texas coast. Whooping cranes use a variety of habitats during their migrations between northern Canada and the Texas coast. Croplands are used for feeding, and large wetland areas are used for feeding and roosting.

The Black-capped Vireo (*Vireo atricapilla*) is listed as an endangered bird species. The habitat of Black-capped vireo consists of dense low thickets and oak scrub, mostly on rocky hillsides or steep ravine slopes in rugged terrain. Nesting occurs in areas with clumps of woody vegetation separated by bare ground, rocks, and/or herbaceous vegetation, often in areas with sparse juniper.

The Golden-cheeked warbler (*Dendroica chrysoparia*) is listed as an endangered bird species. The habitat consists of old-growth and mature regrowth of ash juniper-oak woodlands in broken terrain of canyons and slopes, and closed canopy stands with plenty of old junipers and a sufficient proportion of deciduous oaks.

On August 9, 2011, the U.S. Fish and Wildlife Service was notified and provided the required Environmental and Historic Preservation data for this site. There was no response made on the Federal Communications Commission 106/620 filing or any contact made to the applicant, indicating no significant impact for threatened or endangered species or critical habitat. The Federal Communications Commission 106/620 filing is a FCC Internet based notification system to coordinate with various agencies regarding proposed communication towers (Appendix C). FEMA has made a No Effect determination based on the scope of work and existing habitat on the proposed tower site.

12.0 Migratory Birds

Under the No Action alternative, there could be potential impacts to migratory birds because the existing tower would remain.

The Migratory Bird Treaty Act (16 U.S.C. 703) established a Federal prohibition, unless permitted by regulations, to "pursue, hunt, take, capture, kill, attempt to take, capture or kill, possess, offer for sale, sell, offer to purchase, purchase, deliver for shipment, ship, cause to be shipped, deliver for transportation, transport, cause to be transported, carry, or cause to be carried by any means whatever, receive for shipment, transportation or carriage, or export, at any time, or in any manner, any migratory bird, or any part, nest, or egg of any such bird."

While the USFWS did not respond to the letter dated August 9, 2011 (Appendix C), that no threatened or endangered species would be affected by tower construction, the agency has provided general guidelines regarding migratory birds and offered suggestions for avoiding bird collisions. Migratory birds do not appear to be a problem for the existing towers located on or near the project site.

A general description of terrain – mountainous, rolling hills, flat to undulating, etc.: The topography surrounding the tower site can be described as gently sloping with natural slopes ranging up to approximately 4 percent. The vegetation on the site consists mainly of grasses and no trees.

The National Weather Service estimates that fog/low cloud cover occurs 1 out of 7 days from October through May and 5 out of 7 days from June thru September with an average duration of 2-3 hours during the early morning for Blanco County.

In conforming to the United States Fish & Wildlife Service's "Service Interim Guidelines for Recommendations on Communications Tower Sitting, Construction, Operation, and Decommissioning", the proposed new tower will be a self-supporting, freestanding 300 feet tall structure that will not employ guyed wires. It will be lighted per Federal Aviation Administration guidelines. The fenced tower, shelter and adjacent undeveloped areas are not expected to be directly affected. Therefore, it has been determined there are no potential adverse impacts to migratory birds or they will be minimized or avoided. Mitigation measures with the lighted freestanding lattice type tower structure meets the recommended guidelines for minimal impact to bird fatalities.

13.0 Historic Properties

Section 106 of the National Historic Preservation Act of 1966 (NHPA, 16 U.S.C. §§ 470 *et seq.*) and it's implementing regulations, "Protection of Historic Properties" (36 CFR Part 800), require federal agencies to take into account the effects of their undertakings on historic properties. According to information on the National Register Information System (NRIS; http://nrhp.focus.nps.gov); as verified by the Texas Historical Commission, no historic structures are located on the project site

On October 5, 2004, the FCC released a Report and Order, FCC 04-222, adopting the Nationwide Programmatic Agreement regarding the Section 106 National Historic Preservation Act Review Process, signed by the Advisory Council on Historic Preservation (ACHP) and the National Conference of State Historic Preservation Officers and amending Section 1.1307(a)(4) of the Commission's rules, 47 C.F.R. §1.1307(a)(4). The Nationwide Agreement streamlines and tailors the NHPA review process for tower constructions in a variety of ways, including:

- Identifying classes of undertakings that, due to the small likelihood that they will impact historic properties, are excluded from routine Section 106 review;

- Developing clear and concise principles governing the initiation of contact with Indian tribes and NHOs as part of the Section 106 process;

- Clarifying methods for involving the public in the process;

- Providing definitional and procedural guidance for the identification and evaluation of historic properties, and the assessment of effects on those properties;

- Establishing procedures, including timelines, for SHPO/THPO and Commission review;

- Providing procedural guidance for situations where construction occurs prior to compliance with Section 106; and

- Prescribing uniform filing documentation.

The FCC Form 620 is the New Tower Submission Packet to be completed by or on behalf of Applicants to construct new antenna support structures by or for the use of applicants, tower owners, and licensees of the FCC. The Packet (including Form 620 and attachments) is to be submitted to the State Historic Preservation Office ("SHPO") or to the Tribal Historic Preservation Office ("THPO"), as appropriate, before any construction or other installation activities on the site begin. Failure to provide the Submission Packet and complete the review process under Section 106 of the NHPA prior to beginning construction may violate the NHPA and the Commission's rules. This process is not as a substitute for the "Nationwide Programmatic Agreement for Review of Effects on Historic Properties for Certain Undertakings Approved by the Federal Communications Commission," dated September 2004, and the relevant rules of the FCC (47 C.F.R. §§ 1.1301-1.1319) and the ACHP (36 C.F.R. Part 800).

The primary purpose of the FCC 106/620 filing requirement was to streamline and tailor the NHPA review process for tower construction and designate a single agency as the "Central Point of Submission" to eliminate un-necessary delays between the various agencies involved.

The project is not located near any identified historic places or sacred/traditional sites that may be impacted for scientific, cultural or historic reasons. The location is existing County owned or leased properties which are in remote rural ranch land comprised of rugged hills and valleys for the Church Tank Tower Site.

In response to a letter dated August 9, 2011, The Texas Historical Commission indicated on the FCC 106/620 filing, that No known historic properties will be affected and the project may proceed without further coordination (Appendix C). Therefore, the Proposed Action will not impact historic properties.

14.0 American Indian/Religious Sites

Under the No Action alternative, there would be no short- or long-term impacts to American Indian Tribes or Religious Sites.

Section 106 of the NHPA and its implementing regulations, "Protection of Historic Properties" (36 CFR Part 800) and the Nationwide Programmatic Agreement on the Collocation of Wireless Antennas (adopted March 16, 2001), as well as the Nationwide Programmatic Agreement for Review of Effects on Historic Properties for Certain Undertakings Approved by the Federal Communications Commission effective March 7, 2005, require consultation with Native American tribal groups and native Hawaiian organizations (NHO) regarding proposed projects and potential impacts to Native American religious sites.

The FCC released a Declaratory Ruling (FCC 05-176) on October 6, 2005 clarifying portions of the Nationwide Programmatic Agreement (NPA). The clarification addressed situations where a federally recognized Indian Tribe (Indian Tribe) or Native Hawaiian Organization (NHO) has not responded to a TCNS notification, or to the applicant's and Commission's efforts to determine whether the Indian Tribe or NHO has an interest in participation in the review of the proposed project.

The Declaratory Ruling states that once a tower applicant has made good faith efforts to obtain a response from and Indian Tribe or NHO about a proposed communications tower or antenna the FCC make contact with the Indian tribe's or NHO's designated cultural resources representative. If the Indian tribe or NHO does not respond to the FCC it will be deemed to have no interest in the review of the proposed facility. At that point, the applicant will have fulfilled its obligations under the NPA, and the Indian Tribe or NHO will be deemed to have no interest in pre-construction review of the proposed project.

A letter dated July 20, 2011 was sent to the Comanche Nation Native American Graves Protection and Repatriation Act (NAGPRA) and Historic Preservation Office. The letter was intended to notify the Tribal Historic Preservation and NAGPRA Office of the Blanco County Tower Regional Interoperable Communication Projects which include the Church Tank Tower Site.

The Tower Site is located on Blanco County owned or leased property and there are no Tribal cultural and religious sites recorded for the project site that could be identified.

To identify Indian tribes that may have cultural interest in the area of the proposed undertaking, Blanco County filed with the FCC's online Tower Construction Notification System (TCNS) to initiate tribal participation. Approximately thirty-one days after the "Notice of Organizations Which Were Sent Proposed Tower Construction Notification Information," Tribes were also sent letters, faxes, and e-mail. All tribes were notified via the FCC 106/620 filing and no negative responses were received.

There are no Tribal cultural and religious sites recorded for these project sites that could be identified (Appendix C, Comanche Nation Notification Letter).

No further tribal responses had been received, therefore, in accordance with the FCC Declaratory Ruling FCC 05-176, the Tribal participation process is considered complete.

15.0 Air Quality

Under the No Action alternative, there would be no short- or long-term impacts to air quality.

The Clean Air Act (CAA) was established in 1970 (42 U.S.C. § 7401 *et seq.*) to reduce air pollution nationwide. The US Environmental Protection Agency (EPA) has developed primary and secondary National Ambient Air Quality Standards (NAAQS) under the provisions of the CAA. The EPA classifies the air quality within an air quality control region (ACQR) according to whether the region meets or exceeds Federal primary and secondary NAAQS. An AQCR or a portion of an AQCR may be classified as being in attainment, non-attainment, or it may be unclassified for each of the seven criteria pollutants (carbon monoxide, lead, nitrogen dioxide, coarse particulates, fine particulates, ozone, and sulfur dioxide).

Short-term impacts to air quality such as exhaust emissions from equipment, and dust from grading activities may occur during site construction activities. Equipment used for these activities would meet local, state, and federal requirements for air emissions, and dust would be controlled as necessary by wetting the surface of the work areas. The only long-term air emissions anticipated at the site would be from the emergency generator. The generator would only operate briefly while being tested and during power failure events affecting the electrical power supply to the site. Therefore, the Proposed Action would have no significant impact to air quality.

16.0 Noise

Under the No Action alternative, there would be no short- or long-term impacts to noise.

Noise is generally described as unwanted sound. Sound becomes unwanted when it either interferes with normal activities such as sleeping, conversation, or disrupts or diminishes one's quality of life. Short-term noise generation is anticipated to result from grading and construction activities. However, site construction will be limited the daytime hours. Long-term noise generation is anticipated to be minimal and to result primarily from episodic and infrequent operation of an emergency generator at the site. However, the generator would only operate briefly when tested, and during power failure events affecting the electrical power supply to the site. Therefore, the Proposed Action would not generate significant noise.

17.0 Infrastructure, Utilities, Transportation, and Waste Management

Under the No Action alternative, there would be no short- or long-term impacts to infrastructure, utilities, transportation, and waste management.

There may be a minimal increase of traffic during the tower construction. Routine traffic to and from the site would be minimal and would be associated with operations, maintenance, and repair of equipment. Minimal waste would be generated at the site during tower maintenance activities. All waste generated at the site would be disposed of in compliance with federal, state, and local regulations. Therefore, the Proposed Action will not impact infrastructure, utilities, transportation, or waste management.

18.0 Socioeconomic Concerns

Under the No Action alternative, there would not be long-term socioeconomic impacts because the condition of the proposed tower would continue to be maintained to a high standard of maintenance.

Losing the function of the communication tower would jeopardize public safety because communications among emergency responders would be compromised during an emergency event.

Executive Order 12898 states "To the greatest extent practicable and permitted by law, and consistent with the principles set forth in the report on the National Performance Review, each Federal agency shall make achieving environmental justice part of its mission by identifying and addressing, as appropriate, disproportionately high and adverse human health or environmental effects of its programs, policies, and activities on minority populations and low-income populations in the United States and its territories and possessions, the District of Columbia, the Commonwealth of Puerto Rico, and the Commonwealth of the Mariana Islands."

No significant adverse impacts to socioeconomic resources, economic development, demographics, demand for public housing, or public services are anticipated. In addition, there would be no adverse effects on minority or low-income populations. The Proposed Action would benefit all populations in the project service area by providing better communications between emergency responder personnel. The project is located on Ranch and Farm land that is low productive or unsuitable for other use.

19.0 Cumulative Impacts

Cumulative impacts are an incremental impact on either the natural environment or human environment by an action when added to past and anticipated future actions. No ongoing or proposed actions are known for the project area.

The proposed construction of the communications tower would not have cumulative impacts on geology, soil, seismicity, water resources, wetlands, floodplains, coastal resources, wild and scenic rivers, threatened or endangered species, historic properties, American Indian or religious sites, air quality, noise, infrastructure, utilities, transportation, or waste management, or socioeconomic resources. Positive long-term impacts to socioeconomic and environmental justice are anticipated since the project will provide better emergency support to the community. During the construction period, minimal, short-term impacts to soils, air quality, water quality, waste management, noise, traffic, and health and safety are possible

Table 1. Summary of Impacts				
Resource	No Impact	No Significant Impact	Significant Impact	Mitigation/Best Practices
Soils, Geology, and Seismicity	X			BMPs such as, biodegradable barriers such as hay bales will be utilized.
Water Resources	X			BMPs such as, biodegradable barriers hay bales will be utilized.

Wetlands	X			None
Floodplain	X			None
Coastal Resources	X			None
Wild and Scenic Rivers	X			None
Threatened and Endangered Species and Critical Habitat	X			None
Migratory Birds		X		The tower will not utilize guy-wire and the fenced tower will be lighted.
Historic Properties	X			None
American Indian/Religious Sites	X			None.
Air Quality		X		Construction dust would be controlled as necessary by wetting the surface of the work areas
Noise		X		Site construction will only occur during the daytime hours.
Infrastructure, Utilities, Transportation, and Waste Management	X			None
Socioeconomic Concerns	X			None

20.0 List of Preparers

Jim Barho, Emergency Management Coordinator, Burnet County

Cynthia Hood, Assistant Director, Homeland Security, Capital Area Council of Governments

Government Contributors

Kevin Jaynes, CHMM, Regional Environmental Officer, FEMA Region 6

Alan Hermely, Environmental Specialist, FEMA Region 6

21.0 Informational Sources

Completion of this Draft Environmental Assessment included the following:

- Bureau of Land Management, National Park Service, U.S. Fish and Wildlife Service, and U.S. Forest Service (Wild and Scenic Rivers)

    o http://www.rivers.gov/wildriverlist.html

- Capital Area Council of Governments Homeland Security Task Force

    o www.capcog.org

- Capital Area Council of Governments Long Term Interoperability Committee

    o www.capcog.org

- County of Blanco Floodplain Administrator

    o www.co.blanco.tx.us

- FCC Antenna Structure Registration System

    o http://wireless2.fcc.gov/UlsApp/AsrSearch/asrRegistrationSearch.jsp:JSESSIONID_ASRSEARCH=DGcMTxtfQNLVXbJTNZpLWWGPh3SVLJW7GWflwnrXnS3n71HM8pxg!1840754471!NONE

- Federal Aviation Agency

    o http://www.faa.gov

- FEMA Flood Insurance Rate Map (FIRM)

    o http://msc.fema.gov/webapp/wcs/stores/servlet/FemaWelcomeView?storeId=10001&catalogId=10001&langId=-1

- National Register Information System

    o http://www.nrhp.focus.nps.gov

- National Wetlands Inventory

  - http://www.fws.gov/wetlands/

- National Wild and Scenic Rivers

  - www.rivers.gov

- NEPA Summary Report and Checklist

- Physical Resources, Geology and Soils, Agency Resource
  - MLA Labs, Inc., 2804 Longhorn Blvd., Austin, Texas 78758, www.mlalabs.com

- Texas Commission on Environmental Quality

  - http://www.tceq.state.tx.us

- Texas State Historic Preservation Office

  - http://www.thc.state.tx.us

- U.S. Fish and Wildlife Service

  - http://www.fws.gov/endangered/

Appendix A
Site Photographs

Aerial Photo #1 – Church Tank Tower Site

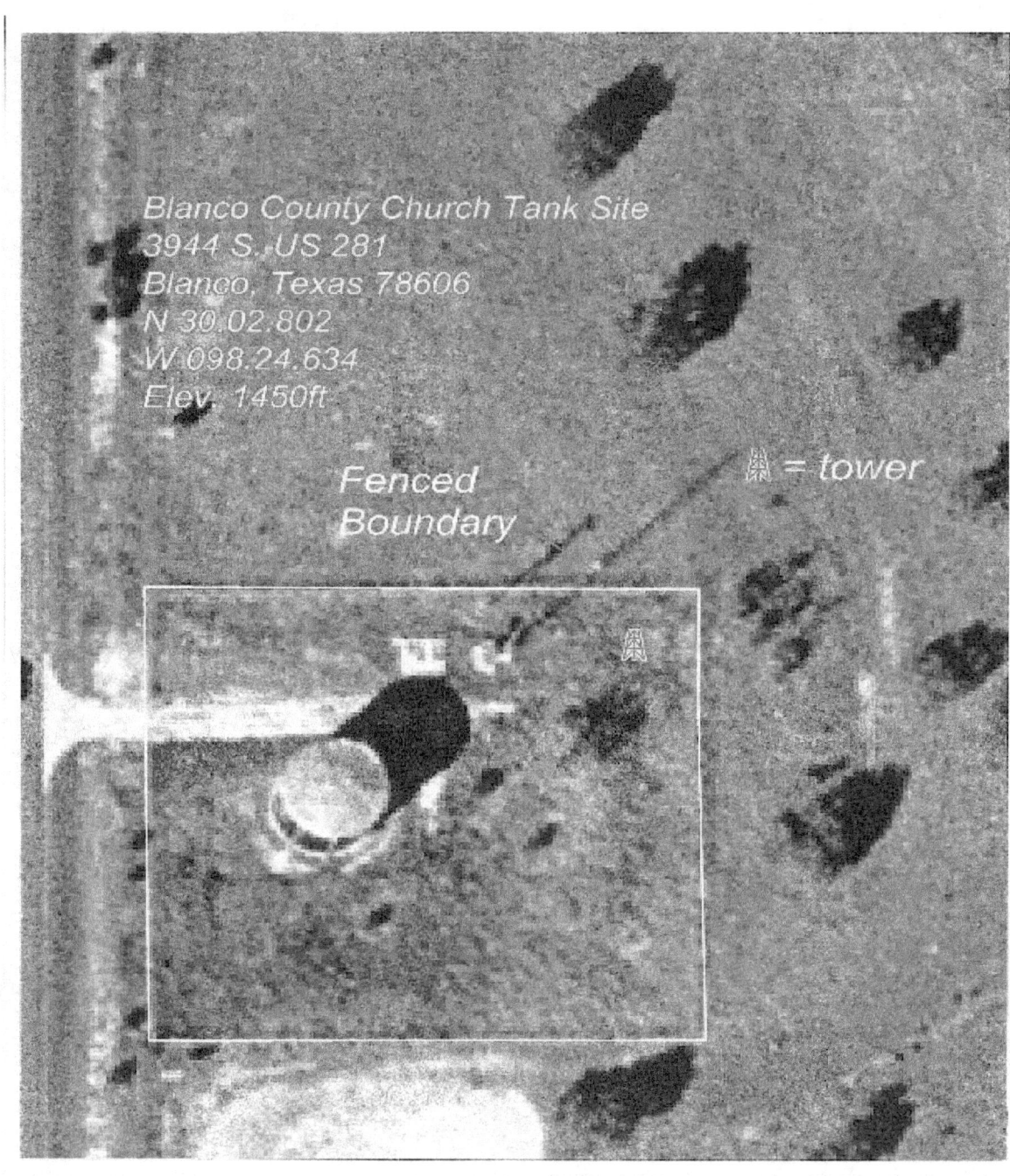

Blanco County Church Tank Site
3944 S. US 281
Blanco, Texas 78606
N 30.02.802
W 098.24.634
Elev. 1450ft

Fenced
Boundary

= tower

Aerial Photo #2 – Church Tank Tower Site

Site Photo #1 – Church Tank Tower Site Pad Location

Appendix B
Site Location Maps

BLANCO COUNTY CHURCH TANK SITE

N 30-02.802
W098-24.634
ELEV: 1450'

Flood Plain Map – Church Tank Tower Site

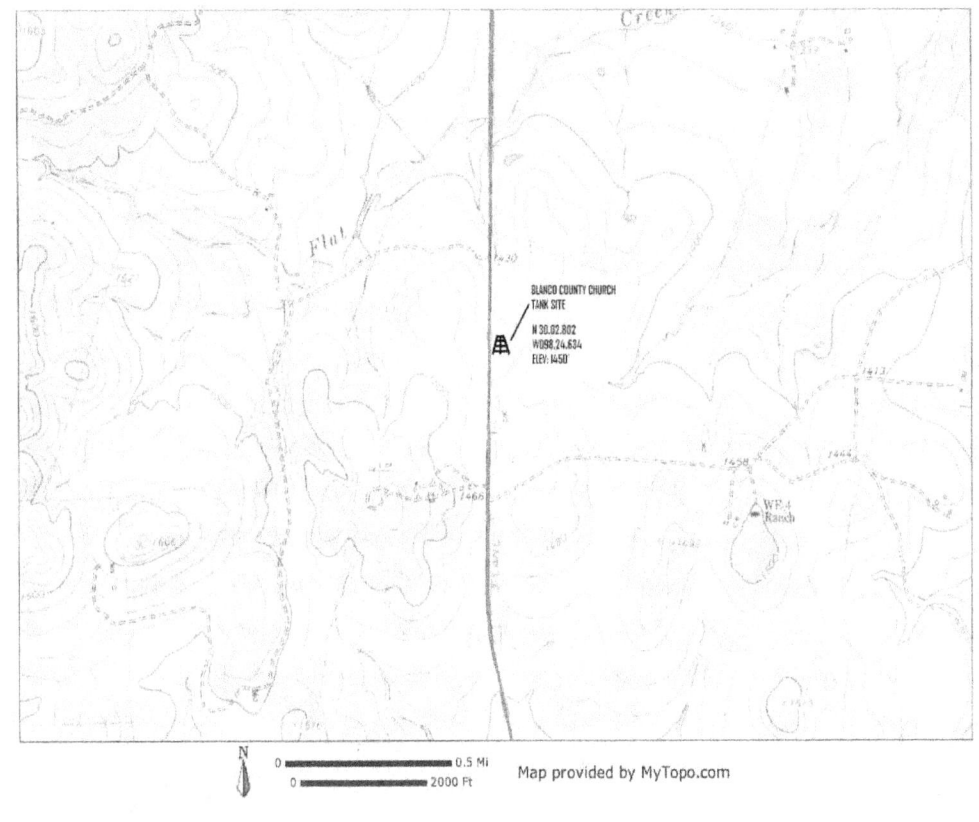

TOPO Map – Church Tank Tower Site

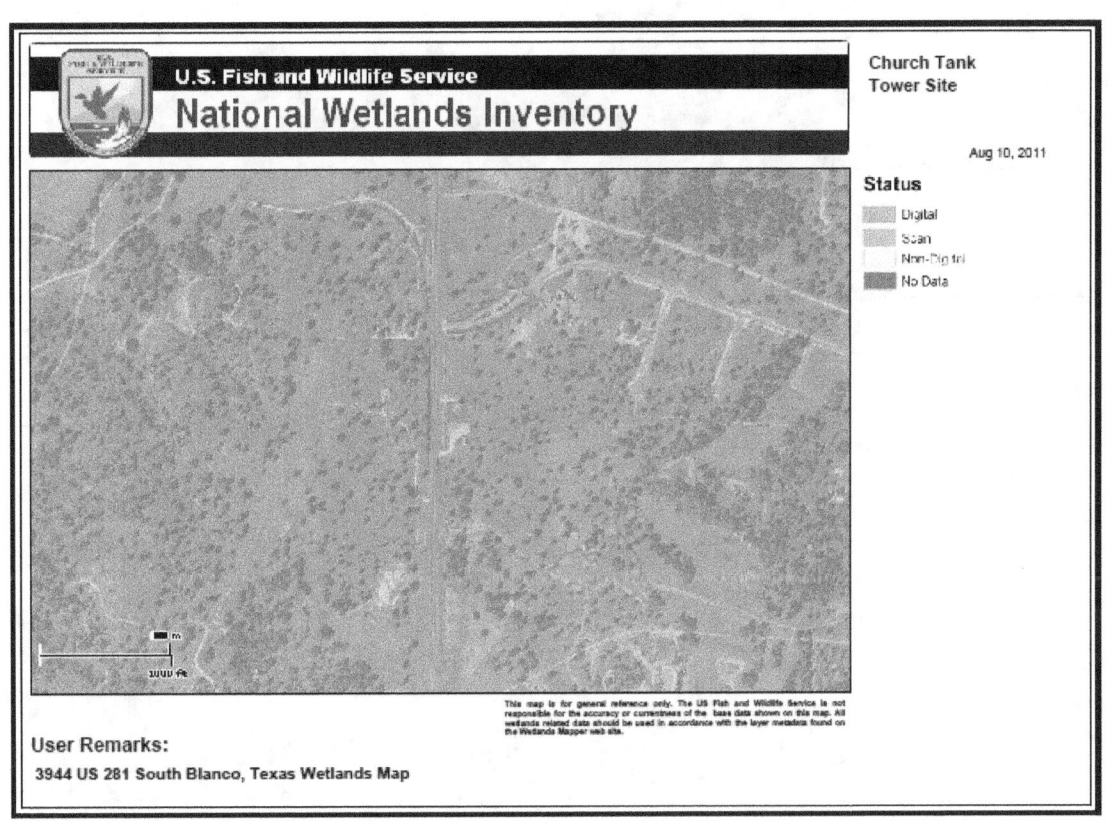

Wetlands Map – Church Tank Tower Site

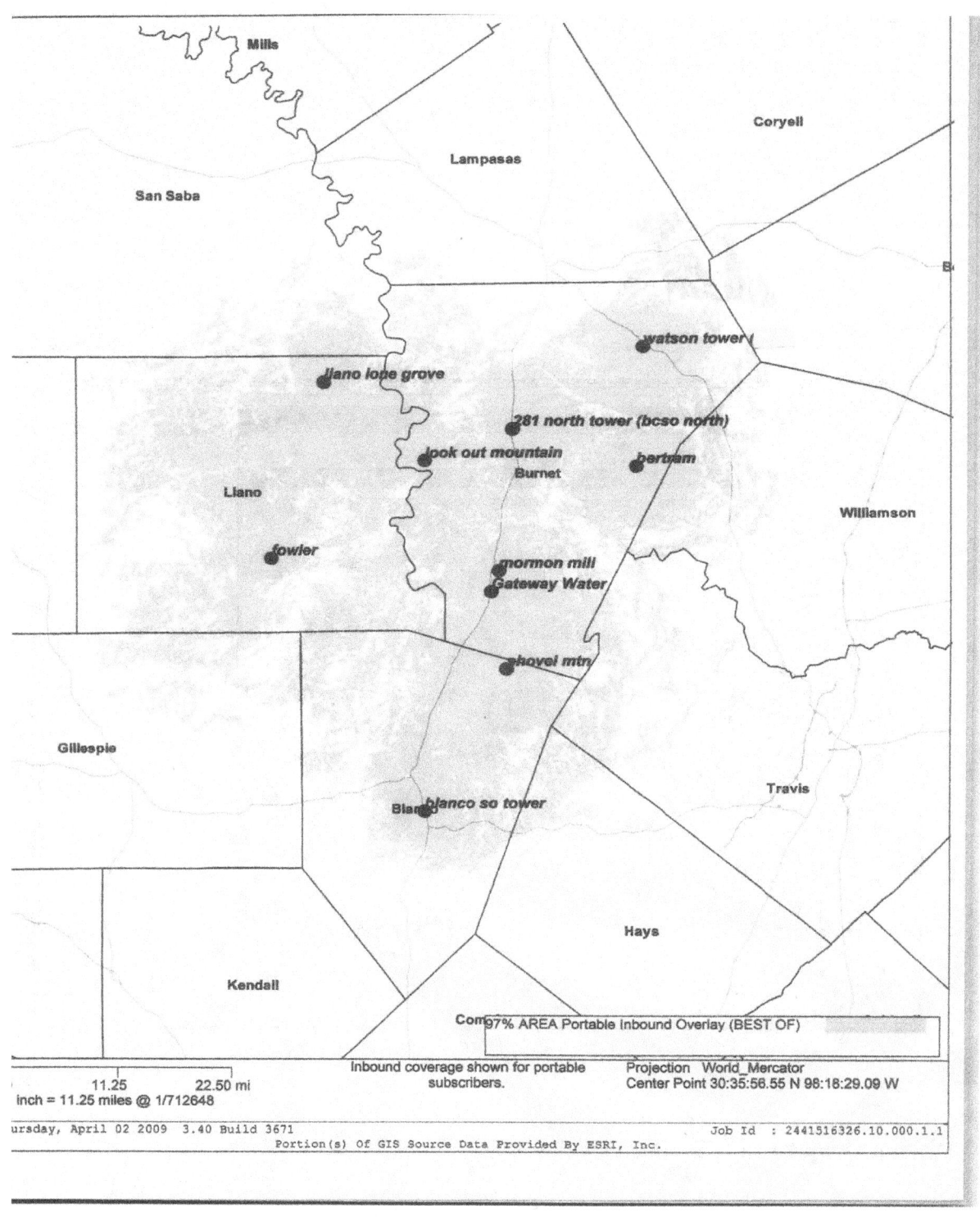

Coverage Studies Map –April 2, 2009 – Blanco, Burnet, Llano Counties System

Appendix C
Agency Consultation Letters

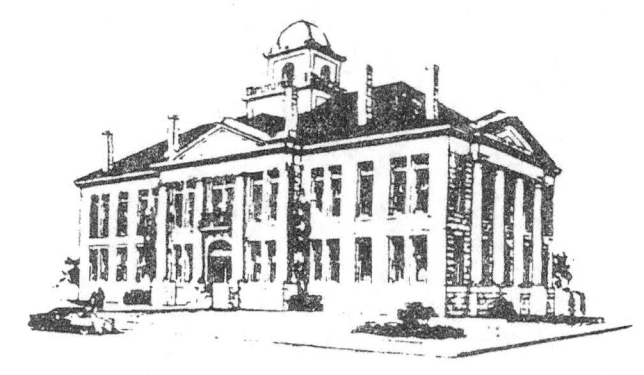

BLANCO COUNTY

JOHNSON CITY, TEXAS

NOTICE OF MEETING
BLANCO COUNTY COMMMISSIONERS COURT

NOTICE IS HEREBY GIVEN pursuant to Chapter 551 of the Texas Government Code (the Texas Open Meetings Act) that a <u>Regular</u> meeting of the Blanco County Commissioners Court shall be held on **Tuesday August 9, 2011** at **9:00 a.m.** in the Commissioners Courtroom of the Blanco County Courthouse located at <u>101 E. Pecan Dr, Johnson City, Blanco County, Texas,</u> at which time the following subjects shall be discussed and action considered and/or taken thereon:

1. Call to order.

2. Consider approval of the August 2011 payroll. Vote on any action taken. (Judge Guthrie)

3. Consider approval of the official reports. Vote on any action taken. (Judge Guthrie)

4. Consider approval of the outstanding bills. Vote on any action taken. (Judge Guthrie)

5. Consider approval of minutes of prior Commissioners Court meeting(s). Vote on any action taken. (Judge Guthrie)

6. Receive update on building project. Information item only. (Judge Guthrie)

7. Consider burn ban. Vote on any action taken (Judge Guthrie)

8. Consider consolidating voting precincts with one voting precinct in each Commissioner precinct for the November 8, 2011 Constitutional Amendment election. Vote on any action taken. (County Clerk/Elections Administrator Karen Newman)

9. Consider relocating Pct. 302 polling location for Blanco County from the old Courthouse Annex at 200 N. Avenue G, Johnson City, Texas, to the Hoppe Room at the new Blanco County Annex located at 101 E. Cypress, Johnson City, Texas. Vote on any action taken. (County Clerk/Elections Administrator Karen Newman)

10. Consider authorization for the County Sheriff to sign a food service contract with Sysco Corporation. Vote on any action taken. (Sheriff Elsbury)

11. Consider appointment of Christopher Voron to the Blanco County Child Welfare and Family Advocacy Board. Vote on any action taken. (Judge Guthrie)

12. **Public Hearing:**
Review of site for Emergency Communications Tower to be known as *Round Mountain Tower Site* located at 862 RR 962E, Pct 3, Blanco County Texas. (Judge Guthrie)

13. Consider approval of fencing proposal for the Round Mountain Tower Site in the amount of $10,892.00 to be paid from Homeland Security Grant Funds. Vote on any action taken. (Judge Guthrie)

14. Consider approval of equipment shelter proposal for the Round Mountain Tower Site in the amount of $20,598.00 to be paid from Homeland Security Grant Funds. Vote on any action taken. (Judge Guthrie)

15. **Public Hearing:**
Review of site for Emergency Communications Tower to be known as *Church Tank Tower Site* located at 3944 US 281S, Pct. 4, Blanco County Texas. (Judge Guthrie)

16. Consider approval of fencing proposal for the Church Tank Tower Site in the amount of $ 4,052.00 to be paid from Homeland Security Grant Funds. Vote on any action taken. (Judge Guthrie)

17. Consider approval of equipment shelter proposal for the Church Tank Tower Site in the amount of $20,598.00 to be paid from Homeland Security Grant Funds. Vote on any action taken. (Judge Guthrie)

18. Consider authorization for the County Attorney to execute a three (3) year contract with West Publishing for maintenance of the existing County Law Library in the amount of $9,804.00 per year. Vote on any action taken. (County Attorney Dean Myane)

19. Consider authorization for the County Judge to sign a contract with the Texas Department of Family and Protective Services for the maintenance of the Blanco County Child Welfare and Family Advocacy Board. Vote on any action taken. (Judge Guthrie)

20. Consider approval of the proposed Blanco County Budget for FY 2011-2012. Vote on any action taken. (Judge Guthrie)

21. Consider authorization for the County Judge to sign an interlocal agreement with CAPCOG for the enhanced 9-1-1 database program. Vote on any action taken. (Judge Guthrie)

22. Presentation of plaque to retired bailiff Harry M. "Mike" Durbin for services rendered to Blanco County. Refreshments to follow. (County Attorney Dean Myane/Sheriff Elsbury)

23. Adjourn.

SIGNED this the 4 day of August , 20 11.

_____
Bill Guthrie, County Judge
Blanco County, Texas

POSTING CERTIFICATE

I, the undersigned, do hereby certify that the above Notice of Meeting, or a true and correct copy thereof, was posted in the Blanco County Courthouse, located at 101 E. Pecan Dr in Johnson City, Blanco County, Texas, at a place readily accessible to the public at all times, on this the 5th day of August , 20 11 at 11:00 A.m. in compliance with Chapter 551 of the Texas Government Code.

SIGNED this the 5th day of August , 20 11 .

Printed Name: M. Kathryn Strickland
Title: Secretary, Blanco Co. Judge
Blanco County, Texas

August 9, 2011

Texas Historical Commission
Ms. Linda Henderson   (512) 463-5851
Historian
P.O. Box 12276
105 West 16th Street
Austin, TX 78711-2276

RE: Submission of Environmental Planning and Historic Requirements for Grants
    For Blanco County Round Mountain Tower Site & Church Tank Tower Site

Dear Ms. Henderson:

In accordance with previous directive by telephone and email, Blanco County is submitting the Statement
of Work and other required documents electronically through our State Administrative Agency for the
Environmental Planning and Historic Requirements for Grants.

As instructed to expedite the FEMA approval process, we are also providing all of the information to the
State Historic Preservation Office and the U.S. Fish and Wildlife Service for their approvals at the same
time as submission to the SAA. We are also submitting a copy to the Capital Area Council of
Governments (CAPCOG) for their review.

Included with this transmittal letter are the following documents:
    1. FEMA EHP Screening Form 024-0-1
    2. FCC Form 620 (Filed Electronic TCNS & E106)
    3. NEPA Checklist
    4. Project Narrative
    5. FEMA Statement of Work
    6. Additional Information for DHS
    7. Certification of Vulnerability Assessment
    8. Coverage Study for Burnet, Llano, and Blanco ALL Tower Sites
    9. Aerial Photos, Site Photos, Flood Plain Maps, Topo Maps, & Wetlands Maps
    10. FAA Determination Letter
    11. FCC Tower Structure Registration
    12. Sabre Tower & Pole Specifications

13. MLA Labs, Inc. Reports
14. Comanche Nation Notification Letter
15. CAPCOG Government Involvement
16. Public Hearing Blanco Commissioner's Court Agenda

We are requesting that your agency review these documents and advise us of any additional information that is needed as quickly as possible in order for us to comply with the FY 2009 Grant Funding deadline. Thank you for your assistance in this matter, and if you need any additional information you can contact me at the following:

Jimmy L. Barho, EMC
220 South Pierce
Burnet, Texas 78611
(512) 750-0507 (Phone)
(512) 756-0247 (Fax)
jimbarho@gmail.com **(E-mail)**

Sincerely,

Jimmy L. Barho

Jimmy L. Barho
Emergency Management Coordinator

August 9, 2011

U.S. Fish & Wildlife Service
Ecological Services Field Office
Ms. Luela Roberts
Branch Chief
10711 Burnet Rd., Suite 200
Austin, TX 78758

RE: Submission of Environmental Planning and Historic Requirements for Grants
      For Blanco County Round Mountain Tower Site & Church Tank Tower Site

Dear Ms. Roberts:

In accordance with previous directive by telephone and email, Blanco County is submitting the Statement of Work and other required documents electronically through our State Administrative Agency for the Environmental Planning and Historic Requirements for Grants.

As instructed to expedite the FEMA approval process, we are also providing all of the information to the State Historic Preservation Office and the U.S. Fish and Wildlife Service for their approvals at the same time as submission to the SAA. We are also submitting a copy to the Capital Area Council of Governments (CAPCOG) for their review.

Included with this transmittal letter are the following documents:
1. FEMA EHP Screening Form 024-0-1
2. FCC Form 620 (Filed Electronic TCNS & E106)
3. NEPA Checklist
4. Project Narrative
5. FEMA Statement of Work
6. Additional Information for DHS
7. Certification of Vulnerability Assessment
8. Coverage Study for Burnet, Llano, and Blanco ALL Tower Sites
9. Aerial Photos, Site Photos, Flood Plain Maps, Topo Maps, & Wetlands Maps
10. FAA Determination Letter
11. FCC Tower Structure Registration
12. Sabre Tower & Pole Specifications

13. MLA Labs, Inc. Reports
14. Comanche Nation Notification Letter
15. CAPCOG Government Involvement
16. Public Hearing Blanco Commissioner's Court Agenda

We are requesting that your agency review these documents and advise us of any additional information that is needed as quickly as possible in order for us to comply with the FY 2009 Grant Funding deadline. Thank you for your assistance in this matter, and if you need any additional information you can contact me at the following:

Jimmy L. Barho, EMC
220 South Pierce
Burnet, Texas 78611
(512) 750-0507 (Phone)
(512) 756-0247 (Fax)
jimbarho@gmail.com   **(E-mail)**

Sincerely,

Jimmy L. Barho

Jimmy L. Barho
Emergency Management Coordinator

July 20, 2011

Comanche Nation NAGPRA and Historic Preservation Office
Mr. Jimmy Aterberry
Director (THPO)
Ms. Kelly Glancy
NAGPRA/THPO Assistant
P.O. Box 908
6 SW "D" Ave.
Lawton, Oklahoma 73502

Subject: Notification of Blanco County Tower Projects for
              Round Mountain Tower Site and Church Tank Tower Site

Dear Mr. Aterberry and Ms. Glancy:

This letter is intended to notify the Tribal Historic Preservation and NAGPRA Office of the Blanco County Tower Regional Interoperable Communication Projects which include the Round Mountain Tower Site, and Church Tank Tower Site.

This project is Phase Ill a continuation of the Regional Interoperable project that has already been reviewed and approved for the Burnet County Phase I & Llano County Phase II submitted to your agency previously. It also has a Regional Impact for regional preparedness and will allow Blanco County to meet the requirements of the CAPCOG Regional Communications Plan as well as meet the mandate of January 1, 2013 P25 communications requirements set forth by the Federal Communications Commission.

The project will assist Blanco County in completing our P25 Communications System for our CAPCOG Regional Interoperable project and is fully compliant with the FCC January 1, 2013 Narrowband mandate for VHF Frequencies that allows for a link back to the Austin Master Site Controller making it an element of a much larger CAPCOG Regional Radio System for Public Safety.

The precise location of the project (latitude and longitude coordinates) are the following:

Round Mountain Tower Site – 862 RR 962E Round Mountain, TX 78663
                    Latitude 30-25-43.1N Longitude 98-19-55.0W

Church Tank Tower Site – 3944 US 281 South Blanco, TX 78663
                    Latitude 30-02-47.7N Longitude 98-24-38.3W

The description of the project, including dimensions/acreage/square footage of structure and/or land affected, with height and structural support information for all communication towers is as follows:

Dimensions/Acreage/Square Footage of land for Round Mountain, and Church Tank Tower Sites are 145' x 85' (12,325 sq. ft.) each or less than (1/3) of an acre each.

Round Mountain Tower Site Height is 320 feet above ground level (AGL) and 1563 feet above mean sea level (AMSL). This is a Self-supporting lighted tower structure.

Church Tank Tower Site Height is 320 feet above ground level (AGL) and 1,497 feet above mean sea level (AMSL). This is a Self-supporting lighted tower structure.

All of these Tower Sites are on Blanco County owned or leased property and there are no Tribal cultural and religious sites recorded for these project sites that could be identified. The Round Mountain and Church Tank Tower Sites are new tower sites.

I would appreciate your review and comment regarding this project as quickly as possible. We are operating with a very short deadline for completion of our Burnet, Blanco, and Llano County Tower Regional Interoperable Communication Projects. If you need any additional information, you may contact me at (512) 750-0507(cell), (512) 756-0247 (Fax), jimbarho@gmail.com (email), or mail to P.O. Box 427 Burnet, Texas 78611. I am also transmitting this letter by fax in addition to electronic mail delivery. Thank you for your assistance and a quick response regarding this matter.

Sincerely,

Jimmy L. Barho

Jim Barho, EMC

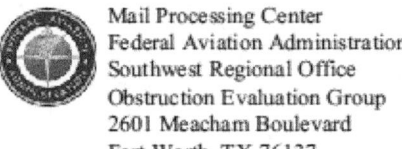 Mail Processing Center
Federal Aviation Administration
Southwest Regional Office
Obstruction Evaluation Group
2601 Meacham Boulevard
Fort Worth, TX 76137

Aeronautical Study No.
2011-ASW-2563-OE

Issued Date: 05/18/2011

JUDGE BILL GUTHRIE
COUNTY OF BLANCO
PO BOX 387
JOHNSON CITY, TX 78636

** DETERMINATION OF NO HAZARD TO AIR NAVIGATION **

The Federal Aviation Administration has conducted an aeronautical study under the provisions of 49 U.S.C., Section 44718 and if applicable Title 14 of the Code of Federal Regulations, part 77, concerning:

Structure:	Antenna Tower BLANCO CHURCH TOWER SITE
Location:	BLANCO, TX
Latitude:	30-01-40.87N NAD 83
Longitude:	98-14-46.82W
Heights:	300 feet above ground level (AGL)
	1497 feet above mean sea level (AMSL)

This aeronautical study revealed that the structure does not exceed obstruction standards and would not be a hazard to air navigation provided the following condition(s), if any, is(are) met:

As a condition to this Determination, the structure is marked and/or lighted in accordance with FAA Advisory circular 70/7460-1 K Change 2, Obstruction Marking and Lighting, a med-dual system - Chapters 4,8(M-Dual),&12.

It is required that FAA Form 7460-2, Notice of Actual Construction or Alteration, be completed and returned to this office any time the project is abandoned or:

_____ At least 10 days prior to start of construction (7460-2, Part I)
__X__ Within 5 days after the construction reaches its greatest height (7460-2, Part II)

While the structure does not constitute a hazard to air navigation, it would be located within or near a military training area and/or route.

This determination expires on 11/18/2012 unless:

(a) extended, revised or terminated by the issuing office.
(b) the construction is subject to the licensing authority of the Federal Communications Commission (FCC) and an application for a construction permit has been filed, as required by the FCC, within 6 months of the date of this determination. In such case, the determination expires on the date prescribed by the FCC for completion of construction, or the date the FCC denies the application.

Section 106 Filings
FCC » Wireless » Section 106 Filings

Logged In: 0021057452 (Log Out)

Help | Technical Support

My Filings | New Filing | TCNS

| File Numbers: 0004833904 | Notification Date: | Current Status: **Completed** | Filer must close by: |
| Form 620: Original Filing | 08/10/2011 | Received On: 08/09/2011 | 10/12/2011, 11:59 PM |

| Update | | Withdraw | | Close | | Email Filing |

| Overview | Transaction Log | Comments | Documents | History | | View Submission Packet | Common Questions | Return to My Filings |

The comments entered here may be viewed by all consulting parties to this filing. Please ensure that comments do not contain information of a confidential nature. Confidential information should be added in a separate document labeled "CONFIDENTIAL" at the top of the document. You must select "Confidential" or "Confidential Tribal Data" as the attachment type when uploading the document.

Post Your Comment

| Submit | | Clear |

There are 0 TCNS Tribe comments

Showing 1 to 2 of 2

1 Show 10 per page (1 pages)

Date Posted	Associated Action	Posted By
09/09/2011	A Reviewer concurred with the filing	Texas Historical Commission

Comment:
The Texas Historical Commission is looking into the missing hard copies after speaking with Jim Berno about this project. Staff members Linda Henderson and Marie Archambeault have reviewed the project through e-106 and find "No Historic Properties Affected," and the project may proceed without further coordination.

Please email linda.henderson@thc.state.tx.us with any questions. Thank you.

| 09/09/2011 | The SHPO/THPO requested additional information | Texas Historical Commission |

Comment:
The Texas Historical Commission is only partially participating in the e-106 system and needs some information in hard copy-- notice of posting on e-106, FCC Form 620/621, map and site photo attachments. We have not received this information on this project so it is NOT being reviewed at this time. We will start our 30-day review period once we receive the hard copy information.

Please contact linda.henderson@thc.state.tx.us with any questions or if there is a misunderstanding about this project. Thank you.

Federal Communications Commission
445 12th Street SW
Washington, DC 20554

Phone: 1-877-480-3201
TTY: 1-717-338-2824
Submit Help Request

SHPO – Approval of Project – Church Tank Tower Site

Appendix D

National Environmental Policy Act (NEPA) Compliance Checklist

National Environmental Policy Act (NEPA) Compliance Checklist

The National Environmental Policy Act, 42 U.S.C.§§4321-4370d (NEPA) requires, among other things, that Federal agencies consider the environmental impacts of any major Federal action. In order to implement NEPA and its associated regulations, G&T requires grantees, pursuant to the assurances related to G&T grant programs, to submit responses to the following questions regarding proposed construction projects. Grantees are required to submit a brief explanation supporting each response of "yes" or "no". Grantees that will undertake multiple construction projects shall submit separate responses for each project, and should consider the cumulative impact of interrelated projects.

Federal agencies may establish categories of actions that, based on experience, do not individually or cumulatively have a significant impact on the human environment and, therefore, can be excluded from NEPA requirements to prepare an Environmental Assessment or Environmental Impact Statement. DHS has adopted certain such Categorical Exclusions in DHS Management Directive 5100.1. These Categorical Exclusions, however, only apply when the entire action fits within the exclusion, the action has not been segmented (i.e., a smaller part of a larger action), and there are no extraordinary circumstances with the potential for significant impacts relating to the proposed action. The purpose of this questionnaire is to collect information from which a decision can be made whether application of a categorical exclusion is appropriate and whether further environmental analysis is required.

Grantees wishing to spend G&T funding for construction projects must contact their Preparedness Officer and submit a request for approval. Each Preparedness Officer will coordinate with G&T NEPA Compliance staff to process each request. Grantees will be required to complete the attached checklist and submit to G&T for approval prior to commencing any construction projects. If, in the course of responding to the questions, a grantee concludes that an Environmental Assessment ("EA") under NEPA may be required for the proposed project, the grantee should submit the EA in conjunction with the responses to the questions, or as soon thereafter as possible. G&T will not approve construction projects until the NEPA compliance has been completed. G&T may independently conclude, based on its review of the responses to the questions, that an EA is required and will contact the grantee to notify them of that requirement.

Requirements on the contents of an EA can be found in regulations promulgated by the Council on Environmental Quality (CEQ) at 40 C.F.R. Part 1508 (and may be found on the web at http://ceq.eh.doe.gov/nepa/regs/ceq/toc_ceq.htm). Note that 40 C.F.R. §1508.9 indicates that the EA is a concise document. It is G&T's intention to adhere strongly to this instruction and to require only enough analysis to accomplish the objectives specified by the regulation.

Grantee: Blanco County
Project Description: Church Tank Tower Site

Question	Yes	No
1. Is the project likely to have a significant impact on a district, site, highway, structure, or object that is listed in or eligible for listing in the National Registry of Historic Places, affects a historic or cultural resource or traditional and sacred sites, or the loss or destruction of a significant scientific, cultural, or historic resource?		x
Explanation for Question 1: The project is not located near any identified historic places or sacred/traditional sites that may be impacted for scientific, cultural or historic reasons. Both (2) of these locations are existing County owned or leased properties which are in remote rural ranch land comprised of rugged hills and valleys for the Round Mountain Tower Site, and Church Tank Tower Site		
2. Is the project likely to have a significant effect on public health or public safety?	x	
Explanation for Question 2: The project will add additional radio coverage to our existing communications for the Fire, EMS and Law Enforcement in Burnet, Llano, and Blanco Counties. This phased project, which is a joint venture between Burnet (1,021 Sq. Mi.), Llano (966 Sq. Mi.) and Blanco (713 Sq. Mi.) Counties, will build a P25 Regional VHF Digital Trunking Communications System that allows for a link back to the Austin Master Site Controller making it an element of a much larger CAPCOG Regional Radio System. The terrain of the (3) Counties consist of 2,700 Square Miles of rural, rugged hills, valleys, and lakes over the (3) three county area. The new system will increase our coverage from non-existent in numerous locations to approximately 94% AREA Portable Inbound coverage. (See Attached Coverage Studies Performed April 2009) This will not have any negative effect on public health.		
3. Is the project likely to have a significant impact on species or habitats protected by the Endangered Species Act, Marine Mammal Protection		x

Question	Yes	No
Act, or Magnuson-Steven Fishery Conservation and Management Act?		
Explanation for Question 3: No significant impact is expected since the project is not located by any bodies of water.		
4. Is the project likely to have a significant effect on a unique characteristic of the geographical area such as park land, prime farmland, wetland, floodplain, coastal zone or a wild and scenic river, sole or principal drinking water aquifers, or an ecologically critical area?		x
Explanation for Question 4: No significant impact is expected since the project is not located by any of the fore-mentioned except near Ranch and Farm land. They will be located on the edge of pasture/cropland that is low productive or unusable due to terrain.		
5. Is the project likely to violate a federal, state, or local law or administrative determination imposed for the protection of the environment? (e.g., local noise control ordinance, requirements for the control of hazardous or toxic substances)		x
Explanation for Question 5: The project will comply with all local planning and zoning requirements that entails the process of meeting these specific requirements for state and local approval.		
6. Is the project likely to have an effect on the quality of the human environment that is likely to be highly controversial in terms of scientific validity, likely to be highly uncertain, likely to involve unique or unknown environmental risks?		x

Question	Yes	No
Explanation for Question 6: None noted or identified to be on record at this point of project process.		
7. Does the project involve the employment of new or unproven technology that is likely to involve unique or unknown environmental risks, where the effect on the human environment is likely to be highly uncertain, or where the effect on the human environment is likely to be highly controversial in terms of scientific validity?		x
Explanation for Question 7: The project is a proven practice for the construction and operation of public safety communications.		
8. Will the project set a precedent that forecloses future options that may have significant effects?		x
Explanation for Question 8: Nothing determined that could cause or have significant effects on future projects of this nature.		
9. Is the project of significantly greater scope or size than normally experienced for a particular category of action?		x
Explanation for Question 9: This project is similar to many that have been completed throughout the (3) counties and our state.		
10. Does the project have the potential for significant degradation of already existing poor environmental conditions? Also, does the project involve the initiation of a potentially significant environmental degrading		x

Question	Yes	No
influence, activity, or effect in areas not already significantly modified from their natural condition?		

Explanation for Question 10:

The natural condition of the project site shall be maintained to the fullest to keep the environmental impacts to an acceptable level.